EXTREME SPORTS EVENTS

TOUR DIVIDE

SUSAN HOSKINS MILLER

SportsZone

An Imprint of Abdo Publishing
abdobooks.com

abdobooks.com

Published by Abdo Publishing, a division of ABDO, PO Box 398166, Minneapolis, Minnesota 55439. Copyright © 2024 by Abdo Consulting Group, Inc. International copyrights reserved in all countries. No part of this book may be reproduced in any form without written permission from the publisher. SportsZone™ is a trademark and logo of Abdo Publishing.

Printed in the United States of America, North Mankato, Minnesota.
102023
012024

THIS BOOK CONTAINS
RECYCLED MATERIALS

Cover Photo: Eddie Clark
Interior Photos: Eddie Clark, 4–5, 6, 11, 12–13, 17, 19, 23, 24–25, 26; Red Line Editorial, 9; Yelizaveta Tomashevska/iStockphoto, 15; Miqdam Balady Muhammad/iStockphoto, 20; Karl Gehring/The Denver Post/Getty Images, 28

Editor: Steph Giedd
Series Designer: Cynthia Della-Rovere

Library of Congress Control Number: 2023939478

Publisher's Cataloging-in-Publication Data

Names: Miller, Susan Hoskins, author.
Title: Tour Divide / by Susan Hoskins Miller
Description: Minneapolis, Minnesota: Abdo Publishing, 2024 | Series: Extreme sports events | Includes online resources and index.
Identifiers: ISBN 9781098292386 (lib. bdg.) | ISBN 9798384910329 (ebook)
Subjects: LCSH: Extreme sports--Juvenile literature. | Action sports (Extreme sports) --Juvenile literature. | Ultra-marathon running--Juvenile literature. | Running races-- Juvenile literature. | Mountain ranges--Juvenile literature.
Classification: DDC 796.046--dc23

TABLE OF CONTENTS

CHAPTER 1

DON'T QUIT

Ty Hopkins was used to riding his mountain bike in all kinds of weather and conditions. But this was different. He was about to start day three of the 2018 Tour Divide bikepacking race. And he wanted to quit.

Hopkins's whole body hurt. He had sores that were getting worse from sitting on his bicycle seat. His Achilles tendon was in pain. He wasn't getting enough sleep each night for his body to recover. The weather was cold and damp. Riding his bike like this was not fun.

He was near Glacier National Park in Montana and had planned to ride this section of the race to the Holland Lake Lodge, a resort 159 miles (256 km) away. Along that trail, he would need to ride up hills that totaled

Riders may encounter mountainous, snowy conditions as well as warm, desertlike conditions on the Tour Divide.

Tour Divide riders pack different types of gear to deal with the variety of weather conditions along the route.

11,405 feet (3,476 m) of climbing. It would take him about 17 hours.

Hopkins didn't think his body would let him do that. He thought he would ride just to the next stop at Whitefish, Montana. Then he could call someone in his family to come and pick him up so he could go home. He really missed them.

Hopkins reminded himself that he had chosen to be in this race. So he decided to ignore the pain. He started to think of things he was grateful for, which helped him to pedal his bike a little farther.

Then the bad weather started. At first, it began to sprinkle rain. The rain soon changed to a heavy downpour. Hopkins put on his rain gear. The rain turned to sleet. Then the sleet turned to snow. Soon the snow became a blizzard. Hopkins could no longer ride his bike over the slippery snow. He had to walk it instead. He also needed to put on more layers of clothing to keep his body warm.

Even with all of those problems, Hopkins eventually got back on his bike. And things started to get better. He stopped at a restaurant for a good breakfast. That fuel gave his body the energy he needed to keep going. The burst of energy also improved his mood.

As he kept riding, he checked his phone for messages. His favorite was from his daughter, Rylee, who encouraged him not to give up, no matter how hard things got. The message gave him the motivation he needed to continue the Tour Divide.

ABOUT THE TOUR DIVIDE

The Tour Divide is the longest, hardest mountain bike race in the world. The 2,745-mile (4,418-km) route begins in Banff, Alberta, Canada, and ends in Antelope Wells, New Mexico. That is at the border between Mexico and the United States. The route runs along the Continental Divide, which includes the Rocky Mountains.

Bike riders go through all kinds of difficult weather conditions while facing rough roads and trails. And they must pack everything they will need along the way. Unlike many other races, riders are not allowed to have support crews follow them in vans with extra supplies and help. They can only stop in towns along the way to restock their supplies. Any bike repairs have to be done at public bicycle shops along the route.

TOUR DIVIDE

The Tour Divide starts in Banff, Alberta, Canada. It ends in Antelope Wells, New Mexico, which sits on the United States' border with Mexico.

Even though the Tour Divide is difficult, many endurance athletes can't stop thinking about it once it gets into their heads. These bicyclists love a good challenge. And the Tour Divide is one of the biggest of all.

PREPARING THE BODY, MIND, AND GEAR

Experienced mountain bikers spend months conditioning their bodies and their minds to get ready for the Tour Divide. The intense training is necessary to help riders face the lengthy course's rough terrain and varying weather. Bikers who have finished the Tour Divide said they trained by riding trails that had mountains and rough roads. They also made themselves ride in all kinds of weather and in both daylight and darkness. Starting with shorter trips, the riders worked their way up to more challenging rides that were longer and rougher to get their bodies conditioned.

To fuel their bodies, cyclists can rely only on food they bring and food that is available to

Rocks, mud, ice, sticks, and other obstacles
can make the mountain biking trails on the
Tour Divide route very dangerous.

purchase along the route. So while getting into condition
for the race, riders must also train their bodies to
accept the types of food they can buy along the way in
convenience stores. Much of that food is not considered
healthy. For the Tour Divide, the primary food goal is to

eat high-fat, high-calorie foods that will supply the body with fuel.

Along with training the body to function the way it must on the trail, cyclists suggest reading everything written by veteran Tour Divide riders before making a race plan. Past participants offer tips on gear, clothing, and food. But a main piece of advice from previous riders has to do with preparing one's mind for the long, hard race.

Rider Cricket Butler of Whitefish, Montana, says riders should "know the reason and driving force behind your choice to take on the Tour Divide. Once you're clear on your reasons, you will find your focus."

Riders also note that keeping a lighter attitude benefited them more in this race than carrying a lighter load on their bikes. Several veteran riders of the Tour Divide have talked about how their minds were a crucial factor in keeping them riding when they were tired or in pain. Some riders were able to listen to audiobooks or music when there was reception on the trail. When there was no signal, they worked to focus on positive thoughts. These things took the riders' minds off their bodies. Matt Griggs, who

EQUIPMENT TRAINING

Before attempting the Tour Divide, riders should practice riding challenging trails with all their gear loaded on their mountain bikes. This will give them experience handling the bike's weight in tough conditions. It is important to know how all the supplies and equipment work before leaving home. This includes practicing with their Global Positioning System (GPS) devices to avoid getting lost.

TourDivide.org has a live tracker.
It pinpoints the rider's location
using their GPS device.

15

completed the 2016 Tour Divide, recommends that riders should "live in the moment" and enjoy the ride.

EQUIPMENT

To prepare for the Tour Divide, bikepacking.com recommends riders start their training with the bicycle and gear they already own before shelling out a lot of money they may not need to spend. It suggests that riders choose a short 20- to 50-mile (32- to 80-km) overnight route close to home as their initial training run. Riders can learn what they need to have along on these experiences. Then they can build from there, trying longer, more difficult routes that require more days and nights on the trail. Riders should work their way up through increasingly challenging training rides to have a much better idea of what they will need in order to face the rigors of the Tour Divide.

Websites about bikepacking and the Tour Divide offer several lists of tips and recommendations about gear. Bikepacking.com noted that the main goal is to have the gear on the bike be as lightweight as possible while making sure to include the necessities. The basics include first aid supplies, a GPS device, bear spray, a bicycle repair kit, clothing, camping gear, and food. Experience in using this gear while mountain biking over long, challenging training

rides will help riders decide what kinds of supplies work best for them before they attempt the Tour Divide.

DANGERS ON THE TRAIL

Even the most seasoned mountain bikers struggle on the Tour Divide. There are many reasons for this. One is because of its length. Another is because of the number of days it takes to ride that far—an average of around three weeks. Additionally, the route takes riders through mountains, forests, and valleys, often over poorly maintained roads. And on top of those conditions is the variety of weather that riders experience along the way. They must bike through rain, snow, and extreme heat. These conditions can lead to slippery trails and deep mud. Additionally, riders have been known to encounter bears and mountain lions on the trail. They must know what to do in these situations to remain safe.

Difficult trail conditions can cause damage to riders and their bicycles.

Cold-weather conditions such as frostbite can cause long-term damage to riders, especially on their hands and feet.

Riders who train for a race of this length run a risk of developing overuse injuries. Griggs says, "Learn how to deal with overuse injuries as they develop." His Achilles tendon began to ache on the seventh day of the race. But he had learned what to do from a physical therapist. By icing and taping his injury, he was able to nurse his sore tendons through to the end of the race without causing further damage to them. Other riders develop saddle sores from sitting on their bicycle seats too much. Any type of sore or wound can become infected if not treated right away.

A RISKY RACE

Another danger is getting too cold and wet from snow and cold rain. This could lead to hypothermia. Riders who realize their body temperatures are in danger of dropping too much must act immediately before the situation becomes a medical emergency. Some signs of hypothermia include shivering, exhaustion, and fumbling hands. If riders become hypothermic, they may have slurred speech and become confused. Without treatment, riders' organs could fail and shut down, causing death. When body temperatures start to drop, riders must get off the trail right away and take whatever steps they can to raise their body temperatures.

Competitors also face the dangers caused by extreme heat. Riders of the Tour Divide experience high temperatures, especially as they get closer to the US-Mexico border. Heat stroke and dehydration are real dangers to riders' health. Riders must be prepared for this weather along with the colder temperatures on the trail.

In recent years, forest fires have presented another danger along the route. Riders may have to detour several miles to keep the smoke out of their lungs.

Extreme weather due to climate change is making the trail more hazardous, as riders must contend with landslides and flash floods. The 2022 Tour Divide had more search and rescue missions than ever before due to extreme low temperatures and snowstorms.

Keeping riders' bodies fueled with enough calories is a constant challenge all along the Tour Divide route. Without enough fat and calories in their systems, cyclists risk what they call "bonking." This is when their energy levels drop so fast that they become nauseated, weak, and dizzy. They run the risk of crashing their bikes or passing out. Riders experiencing these symptoms must stop immediately and consume some calories to fuel their bodies.

Rutted roads on the trail can cause bikers to wreck. And heavy rains that go on for days may cause dirt roads to become extremely muddy. Bicycle parts can become caked with so much mud that they stop functioning. A bicycle accident can result in broken bones, concussion, and other injuries. On the trail all alone, riders may not be able to get help right away. This puts them in even more danger. Riders should seek medical attention for injuries as soon as possible. Some injuries may mean cyclists have to quit the race.

Most riders on the Tour Divide bring along bear spray to fend off grizzly bears and mountain lions that live along

Riders may need to perform bike maintenance along the trail.

the trail. Some also bring along loud whistles and other noisemakers to scare off these animals. Riders must pay close attention to the direction of the wind when using bear spray to avoid the spray blowing into their own eyes.

These are all real dangers along the Tour Divide route that every rider must prepare for. This is not a race for beginners. Cyclists must have a plan for every danger they might encounter along the trail.

CHAPTER 4

MEETING THE CHALLENGE

The Tour Divide does not have any entry fees or formal registration. Riders simply send in a letter of intent, but this document isn't binding. The race begins the second Friday in June in Banff, Alberta, Canada, at an event known as the Grand Départ. Bicyclists take off and start riding down the trails while they are being tracked by GPS. Typically, hundreds of racers from all over the world start. But records show that in many years, at least 50 percent do not complete the race. Riders may quit for a variety of reasons, such as injuries, illness, bicycle problems, or even family emergencies. If riders can't be there on the day of the

Though the Tour Divide is challenging, it offers amazing views.

Many mountain bikers participate in the sport for the thrill of the challenge.

Grand Départ, they can start their own independent time trial (ITT) anytime during the summer months.

Because the course covers so much distance, it can't be marked in any way. Riders generally navigate with GPS devices. A GPS beacon shows where each rider is located. Those locations are plotted on an online race tracker. This is a safety measure and helps riders' families watch the riders, shown as blue dots on the tracker, as they make progress along the route.

THE ULTIMATE TEST

For most cyclists who complete the Tour Divide for the first time, reaching the end of the trail at the US-Mexico border is a reason to celebrate. The Tour Divide isn't just a race. It's a test of a cyclist's physical and mental endurance. It's also a test of endurance for their bicycle and gear. In a race where so

"YOUNG GIRLS CAN DO HARD THINGS"

At age 13, Scarlet Ziegler accomplished something few adults even dream of. She completed the Tour Divide route. She got into bikepacking at a young age, and in 2022 she and her dad set out to complete the 2,700-mile (4,345-km) route. She said of the feat, "I wanted to prove that young girls can do hard things." Prior to conquering the Tour Divide route, Ziegler and her dad also completed ITTs in Florida and along the Erie Canal.

A tandem bike is a bike meant for two or more riders.

many riders drop out, simply reaching the finish line is a major accomplishment.

Riders who have set records in the Tour Divide have done so by sleeping very little. They have ridden through all kinds of weather and road conditions, sometimes riding 18 or more hours per day. They kept riding through pain and injuries or discomfort and exhaustion from lack of sleep.

Mike Hall set a record for the men's category in the Tour Divide in 2016. Hall's record time was 13 days, 22 hours, and 51 minutes. Lael Wilcox set a new record for women in 2015. Her time was 17 days, one hour, and 51 minutes. Jay and Tracey Petervary became the first pair to ride the Tour Divide route on a tandem bike in 2009. They finished the race in exactly 18 days, 13 hours. A new men's record for finishing the race on a single-speed bike was set in 2016 by Chris Plesko. He finished in 15 days, eight hours, and four minutes. Alexandera Houchin set a new women's record on a single-speed bike in 2019 in 18 days, 20 hours, and 26 minutes.

There are no prizes for winners in each year's race or for riders who break the records that were set in years past. The cyclists' reward is their own knowledge that they did their personal best under difficult circumstances. And they endured.

GLOSSARY

Achilles tendon
The tendon that connects the muscles in the calf of the leg to the bone of the heel.

bear spray
A canister of liquid used by humans to repel bears.

bikepacking
A tour by bike that takes multiple days and requires riders to carry equipment on their bikes.

Global Positioning System (GPS)
A system that uses satellite signals to help people with navigation.

hypothermia
A medical emergency caused by prolonged exposure to cold temperatures, in which the body loses heat faster than it can produce it.

independent time trial (ITT)
A way to participate in a race by beginning on a date and time of the rider's choosing but riding the trail according to the same rules as the other riders.

letter of intent
A written document which states someone's plans.

saddle sores
Irritation on parts of a rider that are being rubbed by a saddle.

seasoned
Highly experienced.

BOOKS

Abdo, Kenny. *Mountain Bikes*. Minneapolis, MN: Abdo Publishing, 2018.

Hogan, Christa C. *Mountain Biking*. Minneapolis, MN: Abdo Publishing, 2020.

Vernon, Jane. *Montana*. Minneapolis, MN: Abdo Publishing, 2023.

ONLINE RESOURCES

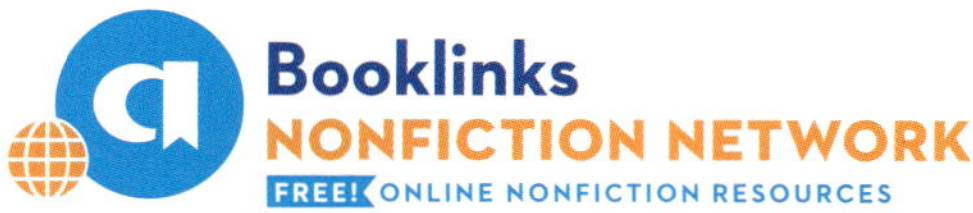

To learn more about the Tour Divide, please visit **abdobooklinks.com** or scan this QR code. These links are routinely monitored and updated to provide the most current information available.

INDEX

ABOUT THE AUTHOR

Susan Hoskins Miller is an Indiana-based journalist who writes for newspapers, magazines, blogs, and book publishers. She works part-time in a university library and is cofounder of Brick Street Poetry, Inc.